Awakening the Cosmic Compass:

A Spiritual Guide to Inner Navigation

Chapter 1: Debunking Myths About Spirituality

———

"Your vision will become clear only when you can look into your own heart. Who looks outside, dreams; who looks inside, awakes." – Carl Jung

I grew up associating spirituality with mystical figures, strict rules and arcane rituals. It seemed complex and esoteric – something for saints and sages, not regular people with jobs and families like my parents. But everything changed when I experienced that magical sunrise at Machu Picchu...

In this transformative moment, I felt absolute peace, oneness with nature, and clarity about my purpose. I realized spirituality had nothing to do with adhering to dogmas or being a "good person". It was about self-awareness, living authentically and cultivating meaning and inner freedom. The mystical was practical after all!

This chapter debunks common myths around spirituality so you can approach it free of assumptions as the unique journey of exploring your soul. Let's examine what spirituality is and isn't before starting tips to make it a part of regular life.

Myth 1: Spirituality Requires Leaving Regular Life

Reality: You Don't Have to Retreat from Life to Be Spiritual

Myth 2: It Means Following Rigid Rules and Rituals

Reality: Spirituality Emerges From Your Unique Experiences

Myth 3: It Requires Having Mystical Experiences

Reality: Small Everyday Moments of Awe Are Spiritual Too

Myth 4: Spirituality Means Becoming Perfect

Reality: It's a Lifelong Process of Growth Not Perfection...

Myth 1 Debunked: Spirituality Does Not Require Leaving Regular
Life

The image of meditating monks, nuns and gurus often makes us think spiritual awakening requires retreating completely from regular life. This perception deters many from exploring their spiritual self while handling jobs, families and mundane routines. We assume the mystical
.to be exclusive from the practical

I learned this hard separation is false. Spirituality is not limited to full-time practitioners but can become an enhancing dimension across
.everyday experience

Consider Amir, a banker and father of two In Miami. He starts and
...ends each day sitting calmly, focusing on his breath

THE FIRST STEP IS THE inner journey - slowly developing presence by training your consciousness. Spiritual techniques are merely tools to generate insights about who you really are beneath
. social conditioning and inherited beliefs

Try this 1-minute Self Check-In every hour

Pause whatever activity had your engrossed and bring gentle awareness to this moment. Scan through your bodily sensations...Notice sights, smells, sounds around you without getting caught up in them...Like coming up for fresh air, check-in with yourself. Allow any emotions stirring to just be. See them pass like clouds. Return to the calm ocean
.of your essence

INTEGRATING SUCH PAUSES throughout mundane days fosters clarity and life feels less reactive. You experience common moments more vividly, discovering spiritual mirrors everywhere .

Remember, spirituality is not a switch - suddenly leaving behind regular life for a monastery! It is a gradual training of consciousness to Infuse daily activities with presence.

Myth 2 Debunked: Spirituality is Not Rigid Rules and Rituals

Rigorous rituals, harsh penance and restrictive regulations might appear necessary for those seeking the spiritual path. Some Eastern or traditional practices seem defined by such stringent methods foreign to modern lifestyles. We assume we must transform suddenly to fit into such discipline-heavy regimes very different from our everyday habits and beliefs .

But the core of spirituality has nothing to do with conforming to an external authority or following pre-defined steps. It has to do with direct transcendental experience through practice. Spiritual traditions offer guiding frameworks but real progress comes from Inner work and unique journeys.

FOR INSTANCE, SALMA was devoted to her Muslim faith and pillars like praying five times ...

THE KEY IS NOT SELECTING a specific pre-packaged doctrine but honing sensitivity. Try varied practices that help develop intuitive intelligence - that subtle inner radar sensing shifts in energy, emotions and consciousness .

Experiment with practices resonating most through gentle self-study :

Creative arts like dance, painting, poetry

Silent meditation retreats

Mindfulness in nature like gardening, hiking

Service roles like volunteering at homeless shelters

Somatic healing therapies like sound baths, Reiki

See which spaces evoke peace, purpose and unity with the world. Then slowly align lifestyle and community support accordingly. Let your . direct experiences guide you, not pre-defined techniques

Spirituality is a unique flowering that unfolds differently for everyone. .Decide your customized path

Myth 3 Debunked: You Don't Need Mystical Experiences to Be Spiritual

We often think of spiritual journeys involving magical moments of bliss, rapture and extraordinary visions. These transcendental experiences seem defining markers of progress on the path – sacred sensations that affirm we are advancing spiritually. Without such dramatic highs of divine ecstasy or unity with the cosmos, we feel our practice might be insufficient.

But the truth is, you don't need intense mystical experiences to nurture your spiritual health, just as you don't need to climb Mt. Everest to exercise properly! Fitness depends on persistent practice – small, simple habits cultivated daily, not occasional extraordinary effort. Similarly, remember spirituality relies on gradual consistency in fueling inner growth rather than sudden mystical explosions.

Consider these subtle but significant examples of everyday spirituality:

• When playing with your baby and suddenly all anxiety dissolves into pure presence.

• Getting lost admiring the northern lights on a winter hike and feeling one with nature.

• Having an insightful chat with a friend where both your masks drop away.

• Finally forgiving yourself for old mistakes and feeling inner burdens lift.

• Pausing to truly notice a glowing sunset and feeling profound gratitude.

Life provides numerous gentle opportunities to connect beyond ego and expand consciousness. Tune into more subtle spiritual experiences accessible in your daily routine without chasing intense highs:

1. Appreciate ordinary moments of natural beauty around you – trees dancing in wind, clouds drifting by. Notice awe emerge in stillness.

1. Observe someone with compassion – a crying child, homeless elder. Feel boundaries between you and them disappear.

---

1. Express gratitude before eating, through prayer or a simple mindful pause. Sense your place within the vast interconnected whole.

RETURN FOCUS TO THE present often. Discover you don't need the exceptional or supernatural to nurture spirituality!

Myth 4 Debunked: Spirituality Isn't Perfection, But Progress & Purpose

Most assume spirituality means becoming perfectly saintly, wise, peaceful and virtuous – models of absolute purity like sages and prophets. We set impossible moral standards for internal progress tied to external actions. But inhaling incense in a meditation hall daily doesn't make you ethically honorable if you lie in business deals!

Being spiritual is not about appearing holy while masking darker emotions and urges. It simply means committing to inner practices facilitative of consistent clarity, purpose and meaning. Expect gradual upliftment over time through phases, not linear perfection.

WITH INFINITE PATIENCE for ourselves, observe inner shifts beyond immediate results or social approval. What truly matters? Not performance but direction and depth of presence.

Keep exploring practices that make you more conscious of how you relate to pain and joy. Turn towards struggles and emotional storms rather than reacting or escaping. Discover the eye of the hurricane... That space holds your power!

Spirituality is a continuous adventure of self-discovery through all of life's myriad experiences. It will have numerous fits and starts as you uncover and integrate new dimensions of your being. Meditate on this – the purpose is not some future point of perfect enlightenment. The purpose is showing up fully in each moment along the upward spiral.

Hopefully examining common myths about spirituality helps open your mind and heart to see it as an inclusive journey available to all. Spiritual awakening is not about radically changing your lifestyle, adhering to rigid rituals or having mystical experiences. It simply means gradually training awareness through practical steps woven into real life.

Spirituality is an inner exploration that enables clearer perception of thoughts, emotions and experiences happening within and around you each moment. This presence and witnessing bring meaning and purpose.

On this adventure, you are the sole guide and authority. Consider diverse perspectives but check all suggestions against your own felt truths. What practices, spaces and communities elicit inner expansion for you right now?

See the spiritual path not as fixed destination but an ever-evolving inner flowering uniquely your own.

Action Steps

1. Throughout this week, pause during different activities to ask "What would make this moment meaningful"? Notice what reflections emerge.

1. Have a dialogue with someone close about spirituality. Ask how they define and experience it. Listen deeply. Notice any assumptions arising to be examined.

1. Sit still for 5-10 minutes daily focusing only on your natural breath and bodily sensations without adjusting them. Just

witness and feel yourself as is. Notice if this centers and grounds you.

LET THESE SMALL STEPS sow the seeds to discover spirituality already present in small joys, simple senses and the extraordinary ordinariness of life! Allow mystical wonder emerge from within your changed perceptions.

The journey promises not perfection but self-revelation if you pay attention!

Chapter 2: Stillness Amidst the Storm – Developing Mindfulness

"If you are depressed, you are living in the past. If you are anxious, living in the future. If you are at peace, you are living in the present." – Lao Tzu

Everything was swirling – my workload increasing as I got that promotion, toddler throwing tantrums with the new baby, bills piling up. Stress was suffocating and I felt stretched too thin like butter over too much toast!

Until one day when chasing after my ringing phone, tripping over Lego pieces while the pasta boiled over, it suddenly dawned on me — I wasn't present in any area of my life. Time to stop seeking outward solutions for this inner turmoil and return home to myself...

This chapter guides you to cultivate a still center amidst external storms through mindfulness – the art of gentle non-judgmental attention to what is arising in the now. Let's distill clarity from chaos!

Defining Mindfulness

Imagine sitting with a curious kid who constantly asks "Why"? about everything new she experiences without labeling things as good/bad...

Her innocent wonder mirrors a mindful state – direct receptivity to each emerging moment just as it is. No filters of past knowledge. Eyes sparkling with interest. Fully engaged.

Mindfulness means paying attention with curiosity, patience and kindness. Observing experiences unfolding with the innocence of a child discovering the world for the first time. Dropping judgement to see clearly. Finding beauty in all – from grains of sand to galaxies spinning...

Now let's move from concept to practice with an exercise. Please pause reading and...

The key to mindfulness is training the muscles of attention – gently returning to the sensations happening now every time the mind gets pulled into memories or future plans. Carrying calm presence from formal sessions onto everyday tasks.

Many scientific studies highlight powerful benefits of mindfulness...

The Science Behind Mindfulness

Numerous scientific studies validate what contemplative traditions have held for centuries – mindfulness meditation unlocks incredible physical, emotional and social benefits:

Reduced Stress and Anxiety

Mindfulness lowers cortisol, adrenaline and other stress hormones while activating relaxation responses, boosting immunity and resilience. Staying grounded in the present moment reduces worrying about the future.

One study had anxious investors try a short loving-kindness meditation before a stressful financial task. These mindful participants were calmer under pressure, made sharper decisions leading to over 11% higher profits!

Less Reactivity, More Response-ability

Becoming aware of our tendency to automatically react helps develop the capacity to consciously respond. Pausing before habitual behaviors like lashing out when angry gives space for making wiser choices aligned with values.

A PRISON PROGRAM TEACHING Mindfulness-Based Stress Reduction to inmates showed significant self-regulation improvement. Meditating prisoners had 37% less substance abuse, 75% less hostility, and 50% higher self-control. Mindfulness cultivated essential skills for rehabilitation.

Enhanced Focus & Cognition

Multiple studies confirm mindfulness strengthens working memory, focus and cognitive flexibility – crucial for learning, planning ahead and goal achievement. Meditators concentrate better amidst chaotic environments.

For instance, Business school students practiced mindfulness before an intense exam. Despite high pressure, they maintained composure, efficiently planned time and scored higher on complex sections involving strategy. Mindfully pausing prevents rushing and improves reasoning.

THE DIFFERENTIATING benefit is a deeper trust in our innate wisdom, diminishing reliance on conceptual knowledge alone. Mindfulness reconnects us to subtle real-time insights guiding optimal flow. We act from a centered space of intuitive intelligence rather than just intellect.

Higher Emotional Intelligence (EQ)

MINDFULNESS PRACTICES teach us to be with the full range of emotions skillfully – not just the pleasant ones. Naming feelings helps articulate inner truths to ourselves and others appropriately. Slow reactivity builds patience and courage.

In one study, mindfulness training reduced emotional exhaustion in difficult healthcare jobs by 50%. Nurses cultivating daily self-care coped better with traumatic cases, serving patients wholeheartedly. They tapped into inner reservoirs of compassion.

Mindfulness boosts EQ – the ability to understand emotional signals and respond empathetically. We move from suppression to healthy expression, from denial to clear communication. Honest emotional exchange deepens relationships.

The common thread in mindfulness benefits is learning to trust the process of life again, restoring childlike faith replaced by an overactive adult intellect. We embrace the present, dropping resistance to what is... this allows natural intelligence to guide optimal decisions that serve the whole, not just immediate gratification.

Now that you see powerful scientific support for ancient wisdom about mindfulness, are you inspired to skillfully awaken presence amidst modern busy-ness?

Brain Training for Everyday Mindfulness

The key is patiently practicing in small ways through routine activities before expanding to longer sessions. Mindfulness takes root through repetition versus perfect one-off attempts!

HERE ARE 3 SIMPLE WAYS to slip mindfulness into daily tasks:

Waiting Well

WAITING ANXIOUSLY STEALS our spirit while buses, appointments or websites take time. The next instance you are made to wait – at traffic lights, checkout counters, phone customer service – relax into it. Sense into the body patiently, listen to ambient sounds, notice surroundings more deeply, without annoyance. Breathe consciously rather than fidgeting physically or mentally. See how this small training builds tolerance for uncertainty and trust in natural rhythms.

Chew Slowly

Wolfing food hastens digestion difficulties, overeating and poor nutrition absorption. Commit to mindful eating for one meal daily this week. Pause before diving in. Notice colors, aromas and your enthusiasm first. Chew small moderate mouthfuls slowly, putting down utensils between bites. Tune into flavours and textures rather than gulping mechanically. This habit bolsters concentration. Digestion improves as you unwind other areas of rushed living too!

Micro-Meditations

Set a phone timer to pause your activity for 2 minutes every hour. Whether you are cleaning, walking or working intensely, stop in your tracks when it beeps. Scan body sensations to release accumulated tension. Take a few conscious breaths. Notice ambient sounds. See if this gentleness helps you return to tasks more fully instead of anxiously chasing completion.

Gradually extending such micro-breaks to 5-10 minutes builds the muscle of intentionally shifting from thinking to awareness mode – returning attention from thoughts about life to actual experiencing of life!

Establishing a Formal Mindfulness Practice

While integrating mindfulness in daily tasks is excellent, it is also helpful to devote focused time explicitly developing concentration. Formal meditation sessions build mental muscles making mindfulness effortless over time. Think strengthening biceps at gym before hauling heavy suitcases easily while traveling!

Find 10-15 quiet minutes and an upright posture. Gently close eyes, relax body, soften face. Tune into the rhythm and sensation of natural breath, not manipulating it in any way. Just witnessing. When attention inevitably gets pulled towards thoughts, sights or sounds, smile and return non-judgmentally to the breath.

Thoughts may share harsh feedback – This is boring! Not working! Just gentle noting of what is happening within and coming back suffices. Avoid harsh self-talk; kindness cultivates change better than criticism. You are patiently training the attention muscle after years of distraction and dissociation.

With regular practice, mindfulness gets woven as undercurrent into everything. Chattering thoughts no longer dominate but become distant noises noticed with empathy but not investment. Daily frustrations – traffic jams, queue delays, slow walkers – don't ignite easily since less reactive. We hold challenges lightly. Equanimity and compassion infuse consciousness.

Advanced meditators achieve elevated consciousness marked by permanent changes in the brain. MRI scans show they activate empathetic neural networks easily with all people, unlike novices lost in fear, prejudice or anger due to isolated egoist thinking.

Lead author of an enlightened brain study astutely observed – "Meditators are free from being a person. They experience life not from the isolated individual's perspective". How liberating indeed!

We miss this unitive transcendence of division in unaware states when we feel separate from apparent adversaries, believing only our view has validity. But meditative stillness lets us penetrate surface perception differences to the singular consciousness connecting all beings. We reunite with true unshakeable power sourced from silent awareness behind transient forms.

Living from this radically inclusive witness perspective transforms how we inhabit bodies, relate to others and inhabit planet. We don't react against situations but recognize external chaos as projections of internal noise. So solutions start from calming our mind clutter. When we sit still and know ourselves as pure presence, right actions flow guided from within.

The epic quest for wellbeing and world peace foregrounds reclaiming now-ness! Are you ready to courageously claim stillness and return home to your full potential? Commit to just one week of daily mindfulness. Notice emotions and behaviors shift – anxiety decreases, patience increases. Small steps accumulate into giant leaps!

Mindful Breathing

This foundational practice centers awareness in the body instead of wasting energy in useless mental spinning.

Sit comfortably. Close eyes. Place one hand on belly, one on chest. Inhale slowly through the nose for 4 counts, feeling the torso expand. Exhale gently for 6 counts, noticing it contract. Focus completely on the sensations of each inhale/exhale cycle. Start with 5 minutes daily, increasing to 15.

Research shows mindful breathing stimulates the parasympathetic nervous system, reducing blood pressure, heart rate and inflammatory stress hormones. Just 25 minutes daily balances neurotransmitters boosting mood, focus and immunity.

Body Scan Meditation

Lie comfortably on back, allowing eyes to gently close. Bring attention systematically from toes to head – noticing any sensations without judging. Allow limbs to sink deeper into the surface when exhaling.

Studies demonstrate body scans significantly reduce muscle tension and back pain by relaxing contracted areas. They also improve emotional regulation, essential for addiction recovery. War veterans with PTSD report feeling embodied and safe again.

Walking Meditation

Find a quiet park trail or pathway. Stand still briefly, feeling feet grounded and body alert. Begin walking at a gentle pace, focusing on the physical sensations of each step. Lift – Move – Place. Feel the wind, sights and sounds without getting hooked into thoughts about them. Return to steps when the mind wanders.

Research on outdoor mindful walking lowers clinical depression by 71% for some individuals, rivaling success of medication. It boosts mood-elevating endorphins and motivation while addressing seasonal affective disorder.

The key is celebrating little steps! Before rushing for the summit, strengthen basics – patience, self-compassion and dedicating few minutes to nurture stillness even on busy days. Make friends with the present moment instead of escaping into constant stimulus. Soon you'll walk, work, create from a space of abundant inner silence! This consolidates any external success.

Modern life pulls us perpetually into an anxiously imagined future while burying unresolved emotions from the past. We rarely pause to ask – How do I feel right now? We urgently react rather than responding consciously.

Mindfulness practice offers time-tested wisdom to return to the peace of the present moment instead of getting tangled in thoughts. By training the mind to pay attention with patience instead of judgement, we realize inner stillness is always accessible amidst external chaos.

Consistent mindfulness reshapes neural pathways that govern perception, resilience, relationships and creativity. Instead of reflex reactions, we learn to respond empathetically. We flow through life guided by intuition instead of just attempting to intellectually control everything.

Stillness leads to right action. Inner quiet allows us to hear the soft voice of truth guiding wise choices. All spiritual trails converge at the summit of presence, hidden in plain sight!

Onward Exploration

1. Observe when reactions get triggered and how long negativity lingers without conscious intervention. Then mindfully lean into tension areas as opportunities for growth.

1. Set phone reminders randomly throughout your week. Each time it beeps, pause and take 5 conscious breaths before proceeding to anchor awareness.

---

1. Notice everyday behaviors done mechanically without presence like eating, walking or chatting. Invite full

engagement by appreciating sensory details.

CHOOSE MINDFULNESS over multi-tasking. The more impatient we get, the slower life's wisdom reveals itself to guide miracles! Experiment with active surrender beyond willpower. Allow intuition to flow through your being and right action emerges effortlessly.

May your journey of awakening unfold gently, lighting up the world!

Chapter 3: Excavating Your True Self – The Journey Inward

"Your visions will become clear only when you can look into your own heart. Who looks outside, dreams; who looks inside, awakens." – Carl Jung

I always considered myself an "authentic person" – embracing quirks, ignoring trends and pursuing individual passions. But it took a health crisis in my late 30s to expose the ways I still performed various identities unconsciously – people pleaser at home, alpha executive in office, fun friend when socializing. I had no clue who the real "I" was under these crisscrossing masks!

It took courage to admit I routinely betrayed my core values and truths to conform, avoid conflict or chase validation. The spiritual awakening occurred when I committed to knowing my whole self beyond inherited notions and mental concepts. When we silence external noise long enough, inner wisdom emerges to guide authentic living...

This chapter provides insights and practices to help you uncover your unique essence. Let's journey inward together!

Clarifying Core Values

Values represent our deepest convictions about what provides life meaning, drives priorities and motivates actions. But we rarely pause to articulate them consciously.

Clarity about values requires radical self-honesty. Go within, beyond chasing pleasure or public approval, to understand your essence. What truly matters to you?

For example, Michelle was raised to believe fame and fortune manifested worthiness. But a dark period of emptiness and addiction after achieving outward success clarified her actual core drivers – creativity, community and authentic self-expression.

Take time reflecting on peak memories of joy, painful regrets, mentors who inspired you and moments expressing true self without inhibition. What common threads bind them? Coalesce insights into 5-6 value words most vital to your spirit – forgiveness, dedication, integrity, growth, etc.

Now review recent decisions through this values lens. Do actions align or betray core drivers? Any relationships/goals to reassess? Use this blueprint going forward when confused or overwhelmed. Values serve as lighthouse anchoring direction when severely tested.

Accessing Emotional Wisdom

Emotions convey crucial data about our deep beliefs and needs. But conditioned to view feelings as irrational, we silence messages meant for self-understanding and healing. Reconnect to emotional wisdom within through:

Journaling – Writing freely uncovers insights and patterns about anger triggers, shame stories or pervasive anxieties. Physically articulating fears diminishes their power, opening space for compassion and responsibility.

Artistic Expression – Channel confusing emotions into poems, songs, paintings. Creative avenues unlock nuances Mental analysis misses. No judging the outcome, just be in generous flow. See what emerges to provide clues for growth and reconciliation.

Somatic Work – Methods like yoga, dance, breath work and massage access stored sensations and traumas trapped beneath conscious awareness as muscle tension or cellular contraction. Help release these physically first before attempting talk therapy.

No emotion is the enemy if listened to fully. Befriend your entire spectrum for balanced functioning.

Discerning True Calling

Getting clarity on passions and talents that energize us helps align vocational efforts more meaningfully. Tuning into the types of activities, environments and topics that unlock enthusiasm, creativity and service guides impactful work.

But family expectations, social status and practical considerations often override intrinsic joys when choosing careers. We dismiss whispers within promising fulfillment by following secure scripted paths.

Have you consciously explored alternatives aligning inherent purpose with paid work? Mindfulness practices from Chapter 2 helped Julio, a banker, realize his true calling – youth mentoring. Weekend coaching youth at risk fulfilled him vastly more than corporate meetings. It took courage but transitioning vocations despite financial risks allowed his gifts to flourish.

Assess What You Naturally Excel At

Review past moments of feeling engaged, motivated and joyful while demonstrating your finest talents. Reflect on repeated external praise, flow states during specific activities, enthusiastic hobbies. What came most effortlessly and was intrinsically rewarding? How do you shine brightest?

Get clarity if current career path intersects your sweet spot. If not, brainstorm small incremental steps to transition towards roles for expressing innate genius. Maybe volunteer teaching music weekends before fully quitting engineering?

You might wonder – "But how will I survive doing what I love"? Beyond initial financial concerns, something magical happens when mindfully moving towards authentic purpose... The universe conspires to help manifest dreams through unseen doors! You attract resources, mentors and opportunities needed.

Of course, discernment is key – avoid reactionary escapes without reflecting. Assess genuine priorities and adult responsibilities before drastic measures. But once clear, boldly honor your calling!

Cultivating Spiritual Friendships & Community

The path of awakening and embodiment of our highest self is challenging to walk alone. We require supportive communities reflecting back greatness, especially when we cannot glimpse our own potential. Friends committed to growth through mutual understanding, not just entertainment provide mirrors revealing internal blind spots and nurturing continual blossoming.

Seek kindred spirits equally invested in the sometimes messy, often magical process of awakening. Connect authentically around life's essence beyond surface roles. Foster regular vulnerability around big questions, not just polite pleasantries. Together, unravel conditioning obstructing your true beauty.

In resonance with spiritual companions, loneliness disappears. We feel held in a larger meaning framework, able to express fully without censorship, disconnection or avoidance when emotions get intense. This grounds us in self-compassion during storms before we get reactive externally.

Over time, self-concept transforms from isolated identity to experiential interconnection with all beings. What we heal internally ripples out to uplift humanity. The sacred world community awaits your unique light!

REFLECTION QUESTIONS for Continuous Growth

Transformation relies on investing consistent time for self-inquiry beyond sporadic insights. We must courageously ask profound questions to unveil limiting assumptions created for safety, approval or avoidance of pain. Become intimate with yourself.

Explore these open-ended contemplations as part of daily mindfulness practice or during calming activities like taking nature walks, gazing at stars or pre-sleep. Allow intuitive answers to gradually surface without self-judgement.

1. When in my life have I silenced my inner wisdom or betrayed my soul's integrity? Why?

1. How would I live differently if I directed my gaze confidently inward instead of seeking external validation constantly?

1. What secrets am I still hiding about past actions/urges I judge as socially unacceptable? How can I develop self-compassion around my humanity?

1. What relationships, possessions or achievements appear essential for my happiness right now? How would my priorities shift if I realized spiritual joy comes from within?

1. If I were fully express my authentic self without worrying about criticism or disappointing others, how would I feel liberating? How strongly do I crave this freedom?

1. When I reflect on the moments I felt most fully myself, utterly happy and connected to a Higher Power/Purpose beyond small self, what do I notice?

---

1. What limiting stories about inadequacy or lack still require healing such that I can allow abundance to flow unobstructed?

CONTINUE NURTURING presence with patience. Even fleeting seconds of connectedness with your true essence will dismantle years of false perceptions. Progress might seem gradual or nonlinear but transformation is guaranteed the moment we commit wholeheartedly to living from the inside out...

You are safe. You are held. You deserve to unveil your glorious fullness – spiritual birthright of every being!

Channeling Transformation Creatively

Writing down insights gained from self-inquiry allows assimilation by the conscious mind otherwise prone to distraction and forgetting. Journaling also releases overwhelming emotions onto paper instead of having them repeatedly swirling internally.

Creativity provides a potent lens for distilling teachings and anchoring transformations we wish to manifest in the external world. Harness your medium – prose, poetry, painting, pottery, music, movement or theatrical performance. Playfulness dissolves staleness when we take ourselves too seriously! Dedicate this week to some artistic exploration:

GANDHI – AS A YOUNG lawyer educated in Britain, he could have easily pursued a privileged career back home in India. But witnessing gross injustice against his countrymen stirred his soul beyond personal comfort or safety. He committed to non-violent civil disobedience for India's liberation from British rule despite arrests, beatings and skepticism even from allies initially. His perseverance birthed a blueprint for activism that inspired future leaders like Martin Luther King Jr.

Teresa of Avila – This 16th century Spanish nun pioneered reform of strict monastic orders shifting focus to social service. Driven by an inner voice she intuitively trusted more than church authority, she willingly faced punishment and exile. Her mystic writings later became foundational, describing the soul's ecstatic union with the Beloved/ Divine in vivid verse that was radical then but echoed timeless spiritual truths.

Arianna Huffington – Boldly leaving a prominent political career tracking to become Greece's first woman president, this leading media entrepreneur followed her purpose championing holistic wellbeing, sustainability and underserved voices. Near burnout herself, she urges redefining success beyond profit or power to prioritize health, wisdom and giving back.

Greta Thunberg – As a 14 year old student, she began quietly protesting outside Swedish parliament for climate action, inspired by teen activists from Parkland, Florida. Despite being mocked, ignored and threatened initially as hysterical by critics, she persevered weekly to spark a global movement demanding her generation's right to safe futures.

Dr V – Ravaged by drug addiction and a suicide attempt in medical school left him dejected, this young psychiatrist felt a spiritual calling to empower hopeless cases using faith for healing. Ridiculed for incorporating practices like yoga and meditation with patients, he persisted. Today his rehab centers that rekindle purpose and community have highest recovery rates worldwide.

The Awakening Activist - Ever since a life-changing ayahuasca retreat dissolved his ego and capitalist mindsets overnight, this former venture capitalist leveraged his network and fortunes to lift up visionary projects tackling homelessness, climate action, restorative justice and ethical technology with a savvy modern edge.

We look for inspiration externally but truth awakens within through courage and compassion. What perceived limitations might your purpose be waiting patiently behind to transmute?

Breath work initiates refer to his exquisite verse as secret manuals guiding experiences of divine union. Yoga teachers share his embodiment metaphors to illuminate subtle reality during Sava Sana. Radically inclusive interfaith centers study Rumi poems to foster tolerance and presence. His words have endured across cultures and centuries because they mirror timeless truths about spiritual longing .across human hearts

Born in 1207 CE in what is now Afghanistan, Jalal Uddin Rumi trained as an Islamic scholar till encountering a wandering mystic who transformed his consciousness from mental knowledge to direct experiential gnosis of the Divine. As he surrendered ego Identities, profound poetry inexplicably flowed through – ecstatic expressions of the soul's rapturous love affair with the infinite Beloved manifested . through all of creation

Rumi reminds us of our wholeness beyond surface identities already fractured by names, bodies and stories constructed as separate self. The mystical lovers dissolve Into the one cosmos dancing In delight, no concept of other. We taste boundless belonging in Rumi's wordsmithing. Centuries before astronauts glimpsed Earth from space, this Sufi seer articulated the radiant interbeing of all creatures in Source . light

In his compassion, Rumi saw beyond sick to sickness. His blessing still beckons, "Come!" to the forgotten, repressed and damaged parts too terrified to consider holy summons. We receive permission through Rumi's modeling to be fully human with each other - inconsistent, hypocritical, betrayed and betrayer each turn, yet eternally held blameless in unconditional Source arms that relax shame, transmute

contempt to empathy. This grace nourishes roots deeper than rightness
.

Rumi urges not blind belief but direct perception of the magical undergirding everyday perception so we remember to live astonished by the Majestic within the mundane. Rumi Invisibly dwells in those unguarded moments brushing teeth, slicing onions, sweeping the porch without commentary... simply experiencing wonder at what is without judgment or chore. That receptivity to Inhabit this "uncontrived moment freely given" softens fixation on drama and problems as the Beloved hides playfully behind conflict and loss, beckoning intimacy if we relax faces furrowed by survival trances... and
. sip tea NOW

Through his stellar solution-less honesty, Rumi becomes our most reliable ancillary guide whenever meaning and sanity seem only faint flickers In relentless madness of breakups and breakdowns. He sits calmly in dreaded gaps between stimulus and response, beholds the Irreconcilable contradictions of humanity with grinning forbearance...no advice to impart but immense sky space to breathe alternate possibilities for responding instead of reacting. And so, rediscovering Rumi inevitably assists recovering wholeness right under
! our noses. He laughs last as splendid spirit that he Is

Rumi's contemporary resonance confirms timeless teachers inhabit all dark bewildering eras to remind future light bearers - you are never separated from meaning, you were never alone on this adventure for wisdom. Death bewilders mortality but cannot disrupt timeless affinity between lovers' souls who meet before bodies manifest. And so In Rumi's magical mirror we recognize self above Individuated cry for recognition, safety, vengeance. Our real name Is Beloved! His illumination calls past preoccupations mere adolescent angst before which grander guest awaits at the banquet prepared behind veils...if

we accept Invitation Home beyond desperately hoarding worldly
. consolations

Through Rumi's provocations, we awaken to the reality illusion. His
words transcend attempts to harness meaning and beauty to serve
selves still seduced by smaller samsaric spheres. He dances free of tiring
Identity trances we cling to. And in that boundless being, Rumi
liberates beauty to inhabit your veins In place of blood, allows poetry
to course freely through messy moments so we walk barefoot on verses
lining uncertain terrain ahead. His fragrant legacy - to boldly bear the
divine fire beyond reasonable comforts, to unbecoming everything that
!is not God

Chapter 4: Navigating Spirituality in Relationships and Daily Life

"Enlightenment must come little by little – otherwise it would overwhelm." – Idries Shah

I remember the blissful high after my first 10-day silent meditation retreat – I felt l bathed in unconditional love, at one with all beings! But returning home, shocked to see my family carry on with usual complaints about work, social drama and mundane chores. "How could they not realize everything is divine consciousness"? I judged.

In my spiritual pride, I wanted to teach profound dimensions of reality to loved ones. Instead, they felt upset by my preachiness and aloofness towards shared goals that bonded us before. Over zealousness created distance from the very hearts I longed to awaken! With patience and humility, I learned integration is subtler...

This chapter shares wisdom on navigating our evolutionary path with empathy, communicating awakened experiences skillfully without judgment and continuing fulfilling obligations with enhanced consciousness. Let's anchor insights gained amidst life's flowing forms!

Spiritual Partnerships: Friendship and Romance

Few scenarios test embodiment of truths like relating intimately with partners and family who may seem far from the same worldview. Their emotional triggers and blind spots will inevitably mirror ours.

When Jada first started meditating, it centers her amidst work anxieties and chronic self-doubt. But her husband Andre poked fun saying, "This woo-woo stuff again?" He enjoyed logical debates not inner soul-search. She resented his cynicism dismissing something uplifting for her. They argued...

———————————

THE BIGGEST LESSON – extending the same gentle patience towards loved ones as we do towards our own growth edges when they seem rigid or limited. Meet people where they are instead of where we think they should be spiritually. Respect each soul's unique trajectory back to Source without forced awakenings!

Navigating this sensitively prevents spiritual paths from becoming reasons that divide families and friends into "us vs them" camps. With compassion, we remain open doors welcoming loved ones when inner stirrings nudge their journey ahead without aggression or urgency.

This sets the tone for the rest of the chapter with practical examples on conscious parenting, bringing spiritual principles into the workplace beyond profit motives and volunteer activism stemming from contemplative insight.

Learning Discernment with Love: Tina's Story

28-year old Tina felt like she was walking on air after an intensive yoga teacher training retreat introduced kundalini rising and deeper meditation. Exciting revelations about energy centers across the body, mystical dimensions of cosmic consciousness and realizing her soul purpose of sharing awakening flooded clarity. She returned to the high-pressured corporate law practice that crushed her previously but now with expanded, compassionate insight to influence change beyond profits.

Coming home, she excitedly described pivotal spiritual experiences to her ambitious entrepreneur boyfriend Jason whom she'd been dating for 5 years. They met while establishing careers so he modeled focus intensely on financial success. But instead of matching Tina's curiosity about subtle inner shifts, he dismissed meditation as "pointless naval gazing, the escape route for lazy people." She tried explaining awakening fueled creative action, not inaction but his rigid beliefs were shut. They ended arguing about Jason's excessive work hours burning him out and harming their intimacy.

Over following weeks, Tina tried gently inviting Jason to yoga classes, breath work workshops, nature walks to provide him glimpses into contemplative spaces so nourishing for her lately. But he stayed stubborn – "overloaded schedules run high-performance lives not this fluffy stuff!" When she persisted beyond his comfort, Jason turned defensive and mocked Tina's ambitions to integrate mindfulness for juvenile inmates. Insensitive comments like "A white-girl wanting to save incarcerated thugs feels like classic social justice narcissism!" left her distraught when she longed for empathetic support while clarifying direction.

After a month struggling through disconnect around their evolving interests and values, Tina realized brute forcing awakened perspectives wouldn't work long-term if partners remained indifferent or hostile. She understood Jason's limitations stemmed from narrowly prioritizing achievements, status and wealth as markers of success impressing peers. His ego attachment simply blinded him to deeper spiritual joy she discovered.

Tina shifted from desperately wanting to awaken Jason towards trusting his innate brilliance to guide next growth steps. She focused on embodying her transformation through consistent, non-judgemental compassion – not just advocating high ideals. Tina stopped pushing Jason to meditate or journal but also firmly held boundaries around qualifying for her support. If he continued dismissing her life purpose as brainless, she withdrew from relationship roles compromise would violate self-honoring.

The paradoxical insight – accepting Jason as he was while fully committing to her own path ahead opened possibilities. Jason witnessed the tangible emotional stability and creativity manifesting through Tina simply tending her inner wellspring with genuine curiosity beyond needing validation. He privately wondered whether secularized mindfulness practices could enhance his leadership skills shattering under ruthless business demands...

Over the next year, bittersweet parting occurred as Tina realized while caring for Jason deeply, they journeyed different arcs at this stage – her towards opening creativity through surrender while his towards mastering external domains aggressively. Breakups hurt but also liberated next phases of flourishing impossible confined through mismatched growth.

In Tina's story we witness how skillful spiritual discernment blossoms by respecting individual terrain and rhythms while watering our own soils. Through observing ego trips compassionately but refusing to abandon essence for any relationship's comfort, we embody awakening. Over time, even skeptics transform benefiting indirectly from our sustained frequency. But that cannot be demanded, only organically attracted by relaxed authenticity, not anxious fervor. We arrive safe alone together.

Spirituality with Family

Heated debates over religious rituals, ethical behavior expectations and emphasis on worldly duties like academics/career choice characterized the dynamics between Tanya, a college freshman exploring Eastern mysticism and her conservative Hindu parents back home. They dismissed her soul-searching through meditation/yoga retreats as reckless rebellion breaching traditions worshipping idols of Kali, Krishna they cherished for generations...

1. Defusing Dogma for Insight

Tanya avoided framing new practices as superior or renouncing birth faith to aggravate family wounds initially. She focused simply nurturing inner stillness beyond rigid steps first. When calmly explaining mindfulness aligning all worship towards truth, parents judged less. Time revealed integrity.

1. Embodying Unconditionally

With ongoing respectful dialogue, Tanya's parents noticed reduced anxiety plus steadier confidence in her even during campus challenges. Though cautious about ritual changes, witnessing positive behaviors countered suspicions. Core family connection stronger than forms.

Workplace Spirituality

1. Lead Meetings Consciously

Rishi recently joined an elite consulting firm after years building sustainable businesses. Challenging hyper-competitive culture focused on increasing profits through endless urgent deadlines stressed colleagues. Rishi proposed starting client meetings with minute of silent breathing to center clarity. Teams tapped intuitive insight more aligned with truly serving needs than ego projections. Even senior partners open to subtle techniques reducing reactivity under demands.

1. Weave Wellness In Workflows

Seeing energetic impacts beyond bottomline created openings to suggest further modules on resilience, workplace fairness, managing conflicts with empathy. What began as minute mindfulness practices organically matured more human-centric culture from inner out.

The essence – integrating spiritual principles at work/home by incentivizing experiential benefits participants actually notice, not just idealistic rhetoric. Lead with patient compassion towards self and others.

In Summary

Navigating our awakened consciousness while fulfilling roles and relationships tests embodiment beyond temporary highs. But perceived dilemmas dissolve when honoring each context appropriately. With ego aside, we serve shared goals while standing firmly in our essence and boundaries.

Being guides accepting where people are, not where we demand they should be. Love flourishes through understanding collective conditioning, blindness and pain instead of demanding instant enlightenment confirming our own. Not condemning human follies but transcending judgmentally fuels our patience and compassion.

With friends used to fun distractions, provide perspectives to uplift joy. In romantic partnerships or parenting, model uplifting communication and unconditional support. At work, inspire excellence beyond profits with mindfulness for reducing stress while optimizing insight. Every environment provides openings for influencing cultural shift through walking the path maturely.

Beyond obvious actions, the invisible influence of sustained spiritual practice privately transforms relationships simply through impact on our presence. When we exude non-reactive poise in facing provoked, relate to opponents respectfully, neutrally observe turbulent dynamics without losing equanimity, even hardened skeptics turn curious. They intuitively recognize we anchor something unshakable behind transient roles valuable to nurture.

We magnetically attract seekers from suppressing inner stirrings through too much worldly distraction and destruction. Our awakened being reminds – they don't require radical salvation (or self-suppression) but simple encouragement to look within. A compassionate smile inviting beyond dogma into discovery through direct experience.

As we balance awakened consciousness amidst relationships and duties, the spiritual outsider establishes common ground. Life becomes the paradise all prophets promised underneath superficial crisis and chaos. We uncover the oasis where journeys culminate...within.

Chapter 5: Ego Transcendence and Shadow Work

"Where wisdom reigns, there is no conflict between thinking and feeling." – C.G. Jung

After my cathartic awakening experience, I proudly told anyone willing to hear – I had unlocked the mystical secrets of the Universe through my brilliant meditation! I felt magnificent compassion for all those "unenlightened" people caught in mundane worries, superiority surging as I quoted profound philosophies. But slowly, unaddressed insecurities kept resurfacing around money, relationships, bodily changes... My avoidance of emotional pain for "high vibration spirituality" left me split, not integrated. Time for shadow work... This healing chapter was thus born!

5.1 What are "Ego Traps"?

Even dedicated spiritual practitioners grapple with subtle inner obstacles masking as progress – what expert teachers term "ego traps". These are tendencies created by the wounded small self that feels threatened by awakened expansion:

Superior Guru Complex: When mystical glimpses inflate ego identification with being the expert "who knows". We get attached to teaching rather than staying a humble student too, open and learning eternally.

Dissociating Bypass: Using positivity or non-dual philosophy to rationalize avoiding emotional wounds that require tender care for integration. Escapism isn't transcendence when bypassing processing needed for embodiment.

Martyr Savior Projection: Getting hooked on rescuing others while ignoring needs for self-care and boundaries. This drifts into narcissistic savior complex rather than practical compassion.

These traps reinforce separation rather than feeling connection with all beings equally. Catching ego distortions early helps avoid much pain downstream!

5.2 The Perils of "Spiritual Bypassing"

'Spiritual bypass' involves pursuing awakening to sidestep uncomfortable emotions, vulnerabilities and pain instead of cultivating insight to compassionately engage them for growth.

For example, Veda chanted Sanskrit mantras daily but refused psychological support for intimacy issues rooted in childhood loneliness. Justin avoided grieving his beloved aunt's passing by hyper-focusing on mystical non-duality teachings saying "no one dies". But anxiety and loss crept up unconsciously.

Though radical transcendence is the ultimate truth, as embroiders in human form, shadow integration cannot be bypassed for sustainable living. Let's xdf explore this:

The risk with detaching prematurely into absolute reality is we start using non-dual wisdom to justify avoiding responsibility for relative human emotions demanding care in this dream-like movie. This splinters rather than heals our fragmented parts longing for reconciliation.

Common Bypass Pitfalls:

* Using mantras to suppress anger rather than understand roots for healing

* Overworking to avoid feeling grief/fear after tragic loss

* Pretending we need nothing/no one because interconnected truth says we already have everything!

Beware not getting so intoxicated in higher consciousness that human vulnerability becomes denigrated as lower falsehood! It's all the one Divine Reality anyway – formless spirit in flowing form! Both hold essential keys for liberation.

The art is balancing non-attachment with involvement, floating free as compassionate witness while participating intimately until we don't separate this. No bypassing but benevolent bridging human and Divine...

5.3 Owning Our Shadow

First, what is the shadow? Broadly speaking, these are aspects of ourselves we find uncomfortable or anxiety-provoking so reflexively hide, deny or project. Light awakening brightens insight into our previously blind spots. But shadows need strategic care for highest functioning. Let's explore the distinct types:

1. Cultural Shadow:

Embedded early through societal conditioning and media narratives around gender, class, race, nationality – causing prejudice despite consciously rejecting bias. Healing involves identifying implicit bias through inquiry, expanding diverse relationships to shift subconscious symbolism through exposure.

1. Personal Shadow:

Formed based on painful past experiences – abuse, neglect, social rejection, losses that fragmented aspects of personality to go unconscious protecting remaining whole self. Requires reconciling trauma, inner child work.

1. Aspirational Shadow:

Our wildest dreams/talents that seem impossible or arrogant due to limiting beliefs about deserving grand success per family norms or societal standards. Dissolving feelings of unworthiness helps unleash highest potential future.

Now that we understand shadow sub-types, here are 3 powerful modalities for conscious reconciliation of darkness into wholeness:

1. Somatic Healing:

Our bodies hold cellular memory of stressful experiences the conscious ego avoids processing. Experiential therapies like breath work, massage unearth insightful emotions to release stored tension.

1. Artistic Expression:

Non-verbal creative avenues evoke raw feelings difficult articulating through just talk-therapy. Active imagination drawings, dance, poetry channel shameful memories for resolution.

1. Lucid Dream work:

Dreams reveal shadow aspects in symbolic form seeking integration for growth using Jungian dream analysis. Keeping a mindful dream journal and noting unconscious projections regularly can accelerate self-actualization.

5.4 Integrating Shadow for Wholeness

"Your visions will become clear only when you can look into your own heart. Who looks outside, dreams; who looks inside, awakens." – Carl Jung

The spiritual path is often envisioned as escaping mortal suffering into blissful light. But wholeness actually involves courageously diving into messiness of human experience – facing mental demons and emotional monsters from the past still coiled tightly around our shining spirit ready for liberation!

This compassionate witnessing alchemizes anxiety, inadequacy or self-loathing by finally acknowledging the gold buried beneath negative narratives. Reclaiming disowned aspects of ourselves diffuses self-judgement while empowering responsibility. We relax grasping futilely for fleeting perfection; make friends with imperfection.

No more fractured avoidance or denial. Just wholehearted reconciliation.

Owning projections out onto others heals relationships. Locating fear and control tactics in the body frees movement. Dancing with despair invites optimism. Mindfully hugging hatred deflates its hypnotic trance. Every inch of invaluable essence gets reclaimed.

Keep dedicated shadow work sessions monthly. Be extremely gentle with language, never forcing catharsis. Set boundaries to feel safe being vulnerable; call in support if needed. Use journaling for continued integration after intense emotional releases. Trust feelings to purge naturally once brought into conscious space. Stay grounded in daily routine.

Consistency with self-love perspectives bears sweeter fruits than sporadic intensity without nurturing integration. You need never again abandon your heart on this profound adventure home to wholeness! We got your back.

5.5 Embodying Awakening Beyond Ego Traps

In the lifelong dance between human and Divine, avoidance of either is escapism not liberation. But most vital is remembering each spontaneous stage unfolds in turn when we release rigid grasping at one static identity, forgiving flow.

Stay vigilant for ego distortions posing as enlightenment like guru projections or spiritual bypassing. Catch them consciously, bring awareness back to balanced embodiment and service. Progress over perfection avoids much pain!

Make friends with the vulnerable one who felt unworthy; help empower their trailing talents now. Accept mistakes as messy maps; keep returning to commitment. Infuse meditative spaces with grounded actions embodying unconditional compassion. Soon you realize every step uncovers Home.

You need not become some airy-fairy saint perpetually radiating only joy and light pretending negatives don't arise. Through skillfully navigating the full human experience – ups and downs held lightly – we actualize firmest foundations for realizing freedom in form and beyond. This cements timeless awakening.

Chapter 6: Understanding Projection Pitfalls on the Path

―――

"The master's tools will never dismantle the master's house" – Audre Lorde

I first met Swami Ji at a sparkling yoga festival – this bearded holy man in orange robes chanting ethereal mantras as the sun rose over rustic tents. I felt magnetically drawn to his expansive energy field...my third eye tingling as if ancient secrets lay coded in the lilting foreign syllables uttered from worlds beyond this. His soothing voice gently unlatched each clenched barrier around my weary heart as I sobbed releasing lifetimes of long-held pain without context. In that very instant through Samji's divine grace, I realized unconditional love!

The next years became devoted to my guru – wearing pendants with his image, attending every higher level shaktipat class to absorb elevated transmission, referring family members inquiring about my obvious transformation. Samji's monthly India visits became my spiritual highlight. But slowly, his cryptic moods, yelling at assistants over minor tasks disturbed me... it culminated when under three female devotees accused him of sexual manipulation, I stood by frozen, denying their painful testimonies...

This chapter demystifies the messy process of separating projected fantasies from realistic assessment in spiritual contexts. Let's walk together beyond shattering illusions towards truly embodied freedom!

6.1 What is "Projection" in Psychology?

As toddlers, we intuitively trust caregivers as god-like figures having absolute power to soothe every discomfort, nurture needs, shape reality around us. Attachment patterns and emotional maps form based on this early imprinting. When childhood environment felt unstable due to neglect, violence or controlling behaviors, our natural impulse to idealize gets suppressed by necessity but stays buried, seeking external resolution.

This sets up the tendency for psychological projection – searching for perfect beings onto whom we unknowingly transfer qualities disowned in ourselves. The spiritual path magnetically draws seekers through its promise of inner healing and mystical connection. Teachers seem like omniscient, omnipotent guides to that regressed child part craving redemption externally. Unconscious projection colors them as perfect guru-god parent substitutes capable of instantly destroying our unworthiness and restructuring reality. Blinds us to their humanness.

Projection also extends assuming group mentalities. Impressionable around perceived spiritual authorities, we easily absorb suggestions about universal truth or global injustice without analysis. Charismatic persona and elevated vocabulary overpowers critical thinking aligned with ethics. We perpetuate a cycle out-sourcing our ability to process complex dynamics inwardly first before reactive external campaigns.

6.2 Why Projection Flares in Spiritual Contexts

Moments of intense energetic awakening during practices like kundalini yoga, shamanic journeys, breath work often generate euphoric intimacy – anyone present seeming divinely aligned to our destiny with messages meant specifically for us. We feel magically mirrored and witnessed (partly true given resonant frequencies attract). But attachment kicks in when vulnerable flow states subside, the very people/modalities that created fleeting connection promising permanent inner salvation.

The conditioned self seeks permanence whether through money, romantic intimacy or peak spiritual experiences. But confused by conflating temporary states with eternal teachers, we surrender autonomy too quickly, ignoring red flags and intuitive nags. Ambivalence gets suppressed for almost superhuman hope in some guide decisively erasing our unworthiness forever...

Stay tuned, projection patterns run deep! There is another way as we build secure inner structures...

6.3 Maturing Beyond Need for External Rescue

The first step is radical self-honesty – admitting where our work dried up, avoiding responsibility. Stop begging invisible forces to permanently eliminate universal conditions of suffering! Take courage to recognize inner fragmentation. Meet suppressed parts tentatively seeking cooperation for sometime. You slowly discover – the feared demons appear rather powerless without the storylines, perfectly patient to be included abandoned extremes. Reclaim wholeness gently.

Of course inspired guides matter, but real change crystallizes through consistent solo work – digging into shadow, examining projection sources, stabilizing healthy rhythms before any fast-track enlightenment attempt or surrendering autonomy altogether as devotees. Reliable integrity shines by giving initiates psychological education on attachment traps and cult influence tactics alongside mystical awakening practices.

Once defining needs and childhood vulnerabilities clearly in present-time awareness without self-attack, we build capacities to internally validate, self-soothe and speak for often silenced aspects that got conditioned to expect external rescues. As we compassionately listen without instantly reacting, hidden resources reveal. We train resilience and grounded responsiveness so difficult emotions become digestible beyond desperate escapes or explosions. We inhabit the very wise nurturing witness we unconsciously sought outwardly this whole time! We radically re-parent ourselves to trust intuitive knowing.

6.4 How to Consciously Withdraw Projections

So what does dismantling projections actually involve when hooks are set deeply in long-held beliefs, communal affiliation and dreamy anticipation? Can we compassionately detach without damaging faith?

1. Strengthen Emotional Literacy:

Build vocabulary and get comfortable articulating the fuller spectrum of feelings beyond just anger or frustration at betrayals. Allow time privately abiding with sadness, grief, remorse, longings – using journaling and supportive therapies to unravel roots constructively without self-attack. Unpack psychological drives, attachments and causal beliefs biasing perception without judgement. Understand relational wounds.

1. Unplug from Tribal Trance:

Examine ideology critically if certain rhetoric pushes emotional buttons sabotaging ability to reason logically or contextually. Balance intuition. Analyze facts fully before reacting. Explore alternatives compassionately. Unwind tight identification by temporarily abstaining from reinforcing stimulus and opinions. Maintain integrity before belonging.

1. Energetic Release Rituals:

If feelings of merger or intense aversion grip mind, use cord cutting visualizations to dissolve enmeshment. Release obsessive pull through mantras while consciously revoking previous consent andIOUs subtly allowing another access into mental and emotional fields via unconscious agreements. Reclaim boundaries sensitively. Send forgiveness to heal betrayals without toxicity. Cleanse spaces.

1. Let Go of Savior Delusions:

Make complete peace with universal messiness – the constant dance of coming together and falling apart, clarity and confusion. See the perfection beyond dramas already present. Drop entitlement around paradise arriving through some ultimate special soulmate or guru exclusively. Allow God's guidance emerge everywhere when attachment to form lessens. Notice awakening reflecting all around in fractal stories once projection withdraws fully back into prayerful surrender.

6.5 Embodying the Inner Master

As projection patterns unwind with care, we infuse trust knowing flawed paths too guided necessary learning. Compartmental obsessions fade revealing wholeness. Blaming self or others now seems comical distraction from instant peace within reach!

The futile search ends. We feel consistency of presence expand into actions aligned with values and spirit service. We embody teachings not requiring compensatory pedestals or perfect vessels. Gratitude outweighs grasping. Curiosity calms rigid reactions. Not some ephemeral momentary high but grounded luminous embodiment....this! Now!

Of course doubts resurface periodically so we compassionately inquire for insight without self-attack. What limited stories or expectations require updating all those while secretly seeking external rescue ? Can we radically revision reality from awakened lens of already whole inner resourcefulness? Are we ready to live completely responsible for our experience yet magically held in divine hands?

Yes this searing path of projection often gets wrapped in tragedy initially before surrender affords the comedy. We courageously change channels through sustained presence beyond fleeting highs. We actualize the living truth as love that never abandoned anywhere.

And so we bow to the divine playwright weaving fractal awakening stories across time immemorial. The inner master reveals behind every seeking mask once we fully claim projections back. We honor the courage of walking this journey consciously together...

Chapter 7: Emotional Alchemy – Transmuting Pain into Passion

———

"You must forgive pain. The ego says, "once everything falls into place, I'll feel peace." The spirit says "find your peace, and then everything will fall into place." – Marianne Williamson

I clutched my face devastated, streams of tears washing down as I screamed "How could you hurt me this way?" Friends tried in vain to console the inconsolable heartbreak of betrayal from the man I loved most promising forever...none could enter floodgates of searing pain exploding every vein in my body on fire...

When a spiritual elder I trusted held gentle space for months of exhausting emotional storms, I kept wailing "will this agony ever end?" Her knowing eyes held mysterious certainty: "If you stop fighting the flames and surrender completely into their purifying depths of shakti...She will reveal your greatest liberation!" Pieces clicked...

This chapter maps emotional crisis into passageways for rebirth. Alchemy is the art of transmuting base metals into pure gold. Let's practice extracting hard-won but luminous wisdom from life's most crushing phases! Your darkest transformations will keep hope sparkling for those still stranded wondering...

1. Common Difficult Emotional Patterns

1. While emotions can feel terrifyingly destructive during overwhelming episodes of rage, grief, despair, worthlessness or panic paralyzing functioning, these reactions represent natural responses to perceived threats for survival. By

recognizing common difficult tendencies within and relating to them compassionately as Wounded parts seeking cooperative alliances rather than enemies to suppress, we can discover their hidden gifts waiting under the pain....

Here are some frequent painful emotional patterns along with supportive strategies for moving through discomfort:

1. Anger Issues: Anger flares as smoke signal for violated personal boundaries and suppressed needs requiring acknowledgment for renegotiation. But chronic heat eventually burns out capacity for vulnerability, intimacy and creativity.

Skills – Communicate needs proactively, self-soothe protectively, channel energy into collective justice efforts through mindful advocacy.

1. Imposter Syndrome: Persistent feelings of inadequacy or fraudulence despite external evidence of competence damage performance, mute talents and block success ownership due to harsh inner critic.

Skills – Recognize critic tendencies stemming from childhood dynamics. Radically accept yourself exactly as is beyond relentless improvement drive.

1. Rejection Sensitivity: Excessive emotional suffering or lashing out when we perceive exclusion or abandonment however unintentionally triggers trauma of original attachment loss. Hijacks functioning.

Skills – Revise core stories of unworthiness, communicate needs non-aggressively, reconnect with wise mentor figures who validate our strong inner light.

1. Anxiety Disorders: Habitual future-tripping from uncontrolled worry-thoughts feeds panic and undermines ability to harness motivation towards meaningful action losing trust in organic flow.

Skills – Return focus determinedly to now-sensations, create routines grounding unexpected change, strengthen faith in inner guidance clarifying major/minor concerns.

1. Depression Pitfalls: Constant self-attack fuels helplessness when flaws seem fixed or supports lacking trapping vison in anguished tunnel without options or agency for problems affecting self-worth.

Skills – Generously affirm self daily instead of criticism to rewire neural nets, list small actions manifesting necessities, welcome support.

We suffer deeply not because we are uniquely damaged but because we share profound heart connection. Stay with the shakti rising from ashes...our alchemy quickens!

1. Psychological Drivers Behind Difficult Emotions

Now we'll dive deeper behind the key psychological drivers perpetuating difficult emotional patterns exploring origins from childhood attachments styles and ingrained neural pathways to core limiting belief structures requiring transformation:

1. Anxious/Insecure Attachment:

When caregivers were unpredictably attentive producing uncertainty managing basic needs, adaptive survival response gets continually hyper activated scanning for safety threats undermining capacity for vulnerability and trust. Perceiving criticism that echoes early abandonment triggers overwhelming flood of anger, fear or despair...

1. Codependent Attachment:

If parents only offered conditional affection tied to meeting their needs first while suppressing child's emotions and talents, unhealthy learned patterns persist – ignoring inner wisdom and limits continually seeking external validation at expense of core values and priorities. This magnetizes unpredictable people pleasing and anger outbursts...

1. Generational Trauma Embedded in DNA:

Often underlying the personal is larger collective context...that our parents and grandparents endured war, displacement, prejudice, poverty. Epigenetics confirm these intergenerational stresses alter gene expression shaping involuntary fear reactions. Healing involves locating historical hurt and enacting restoration.

1. Childhood Gas lighting: Confusing manipulation from family continuously questioning legitimate reactions seeds self-doubt making assertiveness extremely difficult without guilt. Restoring emotional tracking clarity guides secure choices aligned with inner truth beyond external invalidation.

The good news – once traumatized neural nets are consciously identified, we can actively strengthen new empowering highways through repetition of supportive thoughts, exposure to healthier dynamics and embodied practices...really adjusting core perception of circumstances. Aligned neuroplasticity diminishes exaggerated reactions overwriting old defaults. We patiently rewire mental reflexes and emotional habits for conscious cooperation with life's flow.

7.4Alchemical Rituals for Relief

While mastering fundamentals that heal distressing emotions requires perseverant practice, there are a few powerful short-term rituals invoking cathartic release from immediate suffering so we restore enough equilibrium for skill-building ahead:

Heart Salve Process:

Soothe emotional burns by gently placing hands over heart, temples, lower belly with deep pressure while breathing consciously. Visualize divine light absorbing destructive energies until inner child feels calm, protected in your embrace.

Primal Therapy:

Access pre-cognitive layers of long trapped trauma through non-verbal modalities effortlessly releasing stored distress like screaming freely into pillows, destroying pages symbolizing abuse by fire, hitting moldy walls representing what no longer serves. Creative destruction ushers and integration.

Mantra Healing Medicine:

When harsh self-criticism intensifies, chant uplifting mantras creating fertile soil for new beliefs to take roots 'I am enough' or 'I am safe'! Ancient harmonic codes recalibrate neural net disposition across mind/body/spirit matrix held in matrix of unconditional support.

Cry into Mother Ocean Womb

Waters holds profound mysterious power for transmuting emotional toxicity and replenishing depleted life-force. Let waves wash grief and despair from clenched cells while floating salt water buoys broken spirit offering soothing aquatic embrace promising rebirth amidst crashing chaos!

Identify Power Totems

Some emotions seem stubborn remaining impervious to usual interventions. Journeying shamanic ally, we enter mystical landscapes and dialogue with unique spirit animal allies imbued with symbolic wisdom to overcome precisely this cyclic reaction. The jaguar bites anger for assertive communication, owl carries perspective shifting higher truth dissolving anxiety untethered from reality, dolphin lifts depression's downward spirals into buoyant future dreams! What magic messenger awaits you?

1. Channeling Emotional Energy into Creative Purpose
2.

After emergency relief, longer-term updating requires channeling emotional drives into motivational fuel for realizing inspired vision. Passionate expression weaves trauma's severed strands into tapestries depicting how far we've come. What once weighed down anchors us now in common humanity and service. Let's uncover the golden lining for rainbow bridges ahead!

1. Anger Into Assertiveness Training

Rather than attacking unjust authority figures that echo early abandonment and helplessness, practice confident self-expression to hold boundaries now with mentors and rehearse requesting support from safe people first. Role play builds skills to address intimidating workplace dynamics. Forgive internalized repressive patterns by writing petitions for creating more inclusive systems aligned with wisdom values. Redirect heat into solution-building.

1. Insecurity Into Imperfection Art

Film videos joking about personal quirks and upload for empathy exchanges with online communities also navigating esteem issues with creativity. Paint collages of magazine visuals representing negative core beliefs as present wounds and opposing positive affirmations as future potentials to flex imagination muscles weakened by comparison. Have compassion for yourself at different ages and life phases in meditations that relax perfectionist tendencies. Soon novel avenues for molding limitations into unique strengths emerge.

1. Heartbreak Into Soulful Music

Subconscious absorbing songs reflecting yearning for secure bonds evokes deep emotional layers to be consciously felt for healing integration. Music dissolves rigid ego controls releasing flow states where detached witness observes temporary pain without exaggerating meaning as identity. Composing original lyrics helps process relationship narratives more insightfully for taking responsibility rather than blaming exes. What tune pulses awaiting lyrics?

1. Anxiety Into Embodiment Practices

Fear warns of impending non-existent threats hijacking executive functioning into paralysis. Move body consistently to discharge accumulating stress hormones through practices evoking mind-body trust like dance, kickboxing or yoga. Engage in repetitive physical flows while voicing frustration at unknowns. Align actions towards producing necessary resources and discuss worries with mentors to reality check storylines. Carve paths through imagined labyrinths by simply walking with faith.

1. Depression Into Dream Collaging

Cut out vivid magazine visuals symbolizing nostalgic aliveness in the darkness. Slowly craft surreal mystical imagery awakening passion's alienated embers like a luminous futuristic city, magical train transporting inner child to wonderland destination, an enchanted garden paradise growing through tears...Make mini-movies moving through collages accompanied by uplifting music/affirmations! Reinventing reality from soulful visions incubates hope when outer conditions seem static.

Chapter 8: Birthing Your Vision – From Awakening into Action

———

"There is a vitality, a life force, an energy, a quickening that is translated through you into action, and because there is only one of you in all of time, this expression is unique. And if you block it, it will never exist through any other medium and it will be lost." – Martha Graham

I stared forlornly at the incomplete manuscript waiting months for motivation to channel my deepest spiritual revelations into a book assisting earnest seekers. But each time I attempted writing beyond a few pages, an invisible force paralyzed fingers freeze motionless unable to articulate the magical wisdom I clearly remembered receiving in meditative visions! Dark clouds of confusion and despair began brewing around my dream project sourced from such clarity initially. I wondered why divine inspiration flowed certain seasons of tapping cosmic consciousness yet creativity blocked without contextual cause the next day? Grace descended in unexpected form this time as my little niece gifting sparkly homemade cards suddenly animated with unicorn doodles and shaky encouraging love notes...

As I burst into tears recognizing embodiment of my untapped creative birthright in her unselfconscious scribbles, lightning revelation struck – Birthing soul gifts doesn't require complicated rituals, perfect planning or ideal conditions... but simply trusting innocent playful IMPULSE with faith the cooperative universe handles logistics! We forget this magical law of following childlike wonder beyond mental constraints. What dream dares your inner muse? Shall we return to the garden of unlimited possibilities?

8.1 The Moment You Chose This Life

What originally sparked your inner fire before it got covered in conventional roles, responsibilities and limitations from socio-cultural programming about acceptable parameters for "success"?

Exploring past life memories through quantum hypnosis or subconscious womb regression helps unlock soul information explaining foundational forces propelling this incarnation – the seeds of passionate talents, intuitive abilities, purposes chosen for learning specific lessons before being veiled by culturally conditioned identities. This raises self-trust and patience when external approval withers since connection to original excitement burns underneath.

For example, Meena discovered through guided journeying into the planning period before birth that she had chosen to be a female Dalit activist in rural South India in order to uplift oppressed minority women she witnessed suffering enormously in previous lifetimes unable to influence then without getting killed. Her current frustration around creative writing blocks diminished realizing they represented fears of persecution if she powerfully expressed feminine power and wisdom against patriarchal religious norms... Generational spirit trauma requires healing such that her vision catalyzes liberation across castes. Past life recognition dispels present uncertainty!

As we compassionately unearth the originating impulse for incarnating now, meaning frames even painful parts of the path witnessing destiny at play. We remember choosing exact family dynamics, relationships, adversarial life events for burning karmic complexes still echoing across time. Understanding the curriculum selected by soul for maximum learning and contribution helps trust frustrated phases of this birth journey too as necessary stepping stones towards envisioned peaks awaiting activation!

8.2 Your Purpose Blueprint – Unique Archetypes & Modalities

Beyond cultural titles and identities associated with temporary roles, discovering core archetypes anchoring your eternal spirit through multiple lifetimes reveals consistent currents of innate genius, preferred modalities of expression and fulfilling causes fueling diverse embodiments across space-time!

For example, Chang explored his past life visions to realize he had incarnated as...

1) Powerful wizard recluse intensely immersed in alchemical potion experimentation

2) Passionate poet conveying throught provoking mystical truths in verse

3) Monk healer uplifting people's vibrational frequency through sound

4) Metaphysical painter portraying higher dimensional energy fields

This clarified his perennial affinity with esoteric knowledge, creative communication channels and community care service! He thus understood current anxiety around constructor criticism thwarting architectural ambitions connected past persecution for exercising magical abilities or artistic talents condemned under religious doctrine. Uncovering purpose blueprint guided aligning legacy rather than seeking validation.

Try cataloging peak expressions, flow states, praise feedback and passionate interests this birth and across ancestral, cellular memory or quantum accessed previous lifetimes. Connect similar currents highlighting consistent modalities and causes energizing YOUR spirit beyond societal structures. Notice purpose clues fate keeps insisting through mystical winks to nudge embodied manifestation! What

Weaver secretly stitches your legacy whole behind seemingly random incarnations across time? Who are YOU beyond limiting labels?

8.3 Overcoming Imposter Syndrome

A pivotal pitfall paralyzing potentials is imposter syndrome stemming from fear we insufficiently skilled, authorized or influential to catalyze highest visions sourced from soul. We undermine or dismiss inspirations awaiting nurture convinced global impact hubris requires worthier humility denying divine destiny coded in our creative DNA fearing criticism more than courageously risking inspired ripples. But if not you, then who else carries this exact piece completing collective healing mandalas?

We forget symbolic power transcending perceived stature...David defeating Goliath, child leading the way. Leadership means being first to listen inwardly before inspiring change we wish seeing externally. So offer your gift undiluted...if it is bread for one mouth or direction for the lost tribe wandering centuries, stay true to the recipe whispered.

Try invocation below when imposter threats or external doubt triggers undervalue mirror fogging up, cracking conviction about your essential worth and willful talents seeded for planetary betterment:

"Through all darkness and confusion, paralyzing patterns and self-persecution, I solemnly swear my unwavering faith in the miraculous gifts arising from silent spaces where dreams dare my steps beyond conditioned constraints. I consecrate my path to spiritual partnership with life's majestic unfolding however it manifests. By divine hereditary right, I master focus to face fearlessly the unique genius this world requires channeling through my conduit amidst collective awakening algorithms. I boldly authorize my vision sourced from soul remembrance. Into my hands arrives exactly what I need for harmonizing Heaven on Earth as melodies play celebrating solidarity power!"

Say this prayer hands on heart, gaze lifted to skies supporting limitless belief until imposter fog vaporizes as passing mirage unable to diminish timeless solar essence! Your light awaits the world!

8.4 Learning Your Soul's Love Language

Next investigate what specific modalities help you express innermost essence most authentically? We each have unique love languages, modes of processing, communicating and materializing enhanced through particular mediums.

For instance, Marcus found chanting mantras, singing devotional songs and playing indigenous drums accessed mystical states where he channeled profound philosophical insights with eloquent verbosity. However painting contemplative landscapes unlocked higher frequency downloads that grounded through moving meditative dance.

Illuminating such customized gateways to channel sacred inspiration sparks creative flow states exponentially more powerful than generic formulas. Experiment with diverse languages – written prose, poetry, song lyrics, instrumental music, abstract painting, sculpture, fiber arts, mosaic, mandala, mosaic, collage rituals, mystical dance, light language, oracle card decks etc until you identify special access portals where Divine converses through your specialized soul fluency!

8.5 Manifesting Your Visions Imaginally First

Once recognizing the original soul visions and unique love languages magnetizing your juiciest genius, next craft tangible representations of inspired dreams through sensually embodied mediums to solidify direct experiential memory in nervous system and attract collective momentum before physical birthing!

For example, every morning choosing outfit desired to wear when teaching sold-out workshops for spiritual women entrepreneurs, Amanda rehearses receiving applause for upcoming book exactly as she desires fame trajectories manifesting. This daily theatre cements congruent imagination grooves until opportunities magically arrive synchronized those exact dreams!

Try vision boards with stimulating visuals placed prominently, dramatizing goals already achieved through summer theatrical fun, writing thank-you speeches for future awards or accolades celebrating your creations surrendered ego attachment... As Krishna promises in Bhagavad Gita – "Manifesting unmoving from highest goal while allowing means flexibility liberates destined fruits flourishing in right timing"!

8.6 Embody Confidence to Take Action

What still holds you back from bold public offerings despite realizing soul's creative yearning and sparkling manifesting methods?

Unconscious echoes of past life persecution for wielding spiritual power or shame residues around freely expressing the feminine often undermine trust to share our souls publicly beyond private journals/ therapy conversations. Safety fears replay targeting vulnerability.

But cleansing cellular memory of ancestral trauma shadow and reinforcing faith in divine support to skillfully communicate healing wisdom precisely when humanity needs arising voices prevents history repeating limiting patterns.

You were born through galactic convergence and global initiation portals for unprecedented embodiment of mystical truth in action. The masses now stretch beyond looking East/West for gurus... hungry for peers embodying peace and channeling inclusive revelation!

Here are 3 tips for unfurling unique creativity flags with passionate confidence:

1. Entrepreneur Energy Ritual: Envision names/faces receiving your offerings. Feel their appreciation elevating your empowerment in service! Send heart coherence to weave community alliances attracting synergistic collaborations!

1. Ancestral Peace Council: During meditation, visualize elders who overcame immense hostility persevering their truth still applauding your courage now to transcend resistance. Receive their blessings fortifying fearful aspects.

---

1. Pilgrimage Prayers: At sites representing longer legacies like magnificent cathedrals, ancient forests or energy vortex grids, sense timelessness of spirit. Align your modern visions to continuum of conscious evolution. Past lives converge to confirm fated manifestation!

WITH CONSISTENT PRACTICE, embodied confidence unravels past burdened ancestors couldn't attempt saving for this pivotal epoch. But realize mistakes fade, soul seeds persist awaiting your bold planting in collective soil yearning nourishment!

Chapter 9: The Art of Conscious Communication

―――

"When the trust account is high, communication is easy, instant, and effective." – Stephen Covey

I gasped incredulously hearing my best friend Rhea's caring advice on an overwhelming career dilemma mutate into shouting insisting I was delusional for envisioning unconventional entrepreneur paths beyond corporate boxes when single moms like us required security above all!

Swept immediately into wounded rage recalling how I supported her risky art pursuits unconditionally last winter, I screamed back attacking hypocrisy instead of acknowledging vulnerable fears around money and instability provoked by her well-intentioned doubt...

As we sulked angrily for weeks entrenched in self-righteous perspectives refusing reconciliation, I suddenly glimpsed my end of distorted lens magnifying her shadow while blinding mine associated with lifelong scarcity fears projected resentfully without compassion for challenges she faced...

This pivotal relational rupture and repair reflection guides us to understand communication as energetic communion beyond just word meanings, it involves subtle intentions, tone and unspoken layers powerfully shaping bonds! Let's transform relationships through conscious understanding.

9.1 Identifying Communication Blind spots

Pause and reflect – when repeating conflicts erupt in your closest circles, what hidden reactive patterns might inadvertently feed fires instead of increase understanding?

Common culprits include:

1. Unhealed Personal Triggers: Hot buttons around people-pleasing, criticism or discussing money often explode insensitively without context due to our unresolved wounding more than objectively problematic behaviors requiring reasonable boundary setting aligned with care.

1. Attachment Style Projections: Those with anxious/insecure attachment from erratic childhood nurturance tend to interpret even well-intentioned feedback as abandonment signals instead of growth tools provoking dramatic protests or suppressed suffering. Conversely avoidants detached since young infancy bypass vulnerability substituting true intimacy for surface politeness perpetuating inner isolation.

------

1. Neurodivergent Societal Mismatches: Nuanced communication gaps often develop between neurotypical and Neurodivergent minds based on differences like emotional processing, sensory triggers, mental focus, facial/verbal expression fluency and behavioral adaptability exacerbated by lack of societal support or accommodating spaces fostering strengths appreciation.

INVEST SELF-HONESTY assessing messenger projections eclipsing factual message before reactively concluding harsh outcomes confirm suspected worst beliefs/traits in others or world by default! Could compassionate listening shift conflict into cooperation?

9.2 Cultivating Mindfulness and Emotional Literacy

"When emotions get too strong, changing your relationship to them is more important than trying to get rid of them or express them." – Marcia Linehan

Lost overwhelmed in churning rage storms or anxiety tsunamis, reactive habits hijack responding wisely as survival fear floods physiology. Practicing mindfulness returns us from extreme stories overwhelming system back to bodily sanctuary noticing, naming and allowing feelings flow through without exaggerating permanence or solidity of passing weather. Developing emotional literacy vocabulary supports articulating soothed states later with vulnerability. Over time resilience strengthens as we sensitize to subtle inner nuances empowering choice. Daily we rewire reflexes from reaction into response!

For example Leela stopped perpetuating conflict cycles with her hurtful ex struggling with dismissive attachment and substance abuse. Though loving him deeply, she committed first calming hot abandonment triggers through somatic self-care before contacting him skillfully. Setting boundaries against previous patience at all costs dynamics freed energy to uplift other community projects while holding space for his healing. Though heartbreak still arose occasionally, mindfulness reduced suffering by witnessing sadness without drowning within dramatically.

As we befriend the full spectrum of inner sensations from excitement, joy, anger to shame, vulnerability with gracious affectionate curiosity beyond judgment, we and loved ones feel profoundly seen, safe enough to change destructive roles. Over time meditation's gifts accumulate helping transmute painful emotions into creative catalysts instead through surrendered alchemy of presence!

9.3 Deep Listening and Mindful Speech

To transform conflict, both sharing and receiving require mastery – being present with open-hearted generosity listening while wilfully pausing reaction tendencies enough to gather grounded facts before responding.

Active Listening Involves:

- Welcoming whole space for someone without interruption

- Providing listening noises of encouragement (Mmm, uh-huh)

- Gently summarizing content and associated feelings you hear before replying (So you felt angry and hurt when...I'm hearing this matter stresses you)

- Asking thoughtful clarifying questions on areas unclear before conclusion making

Mindful Speech Includes:

- Owning your internal emotional lens framing communication beyond claiming sole impartiality

- Being specific using factual description not general extreme labels while assessing issues

- Talking tentatively expressing perspective as subjective opinions not superior objective facts

- Considering potential blind spots in your own views respectfully

When we lead interacting benevolently instead of habitually antagonizing defensively, truth unfolds.

9.4 Understanding Non Violent Communication

Trapped reacting to each other's quirks frustratingly for years, partners Paul and Nina attended intensive counseling workshops on Non Violent Communication based on compassionate needs focused framework.

They discovered Paul's explosive outbursts stemmed from unmet yearnings for affection and acknowledgement which festered resentfully as hyper criticism towards Nina after long office hours. By vulnerably admitting his sensitive spirit bereft when returning to disconnected environments at home where he didn't feel cherished beyond transactional roles as bill paying provider allowing survivalist lifestyles only, Nina grasped nuances under anger that gentler touch, soothing meals and comforting conversation without distractions could easily nourish, reviving intimacy.

No longer triggered by his coarse communication style, Nina accessed courage to voice her struggles juggling parenting, self care and household maintenance solo most days longing for practical help or appreciation which Paul had no clue drained her energy radically for exhaustively handling domestic realms solo until complaints. Through mutual empathy as their contrasting needs styles clarified beyond bias, they negotiated collaborative solutions valuing each other's gifts through trying seasons.

Compassion blossomed codependence into interdependence!

9.5 Addressing Conflict With Compassion

While conscious relating aspires dissolving reactive patterns before they solidify walls through generous listening, diverging priorities still cause misunderstandings requiring courageous transparency for true heart connection. What principles guide resolving disconnected disputes skillfully?

Conflict Clinic Formula:

C – Curiosity for understanding all sides

L – Listen fully before clarifying

I – Inquire gently about unmet needs

N – Non violent communication

I – Implement collaborative solutions

C – Compassion for growth edges in ourselves/others

For example, when clashing with colleagues over an important work project, Ella resisted habit to harshly shut down her upset teammate aggressively confronting leadership decisions as unfair authoritarianism making him feel bullied. Instead she made space for transparent dialogue where Ella explained her directive intentions coming from legal accountability considerations and strategic planning while apologizing for any oversights causing him to feel excluded or disrespected given workload priorities didn't allow detailed discussions with all employees on micro decisions. Through this gracious vulnerability and willingness to implement more consultative processes for peace, they transformed tense conflict into improved bonding!

9.6 Mastering Courageous Vulnerability

So often we desperately avoid revealing emotional struggles or embarrassing failures to preserve perceived notions of strong unflappable competence critical for securing respect, relationships and opportunities in competitive environments. But without risking authenticity, we sacrifice sacred soul nourishment. Brené Brown's extensive research illuminates embracing passionate vulnerability paradoxically unlocks the very belonging, trust and intimacy with self/others we crave underneath exhausting armored self-sufficiency where gently dismantling walls inviting supportive witnesses becomes stronger than fearing judgment. This manifests opportunities and collaborations aligned with truth too.

As Gloria Anzaldua beautifully captured: "The most potent reward is not the victory but the intimate exposure of the soul."

Exercises Building Vulnerability Muscles:

- Identify your top insecurities and self-limiting stories, write about them openly without sugarcoating harsh self-critique

- Art therapy expressing perceived flaws through abstract paintings for self-acceptance

- Therapeutic inner child dialogue reassuring wounded parts they are now safe and beloved

- Seek communities normalizing tender sharing about imperfections and failures without exploitation

- Take public creative risks – perform songs/poems unveiling shadow, display courageously experimental art

9.7 The Transformative Power of Being Seen

Why does being compassionately witnessed and mirrored profoundly shift our self-worth often more powerfully than years struggling to internally convince our ideal image?

Neuroscience explains human babies don't develop complex identity maps without enough caring eye contact. As adults too, we thrive positive emotional resonance magnifies self-concept cohesively through visible external appraisal indicating internal existence and worth. Cultural storytelling further emphasizes heroic protagonists' journeys culminate discovering tribe sharing higher virtues, purpose and vulnerability beyond surviving alone – exiled destinies remaining tragically unfulfilled.

But how do we attract this soul seeing sacred commune beyond surface bonds? The magnetizing force upholding existence itself is unconditional love! To behold and be beheld as glorious equals, we must surrender misperceptions of separation perpetuating prejudice. Then authentically meet all beings' essence through unguarded intimacy lifting temporary veils. During transcendental exchanges with loved ones, community circles, diverse crowds and nature herself, commonly realize glowing beings awaiting respectful unveiling reside already awakened behind feared strangers or adversaries. As great spiritual teacher Thich Nhat Han observed wisely, "When you can look deeply into your own eyes and see your ancestors, you are free. You know you have a long past and your roots go deep into human life."

In admiring flower or enemy thus, mystics model bridging split lens filtering unity. All human healing culminates sacred communion where another self we thought least likely becomes compassionate mirror revealing our wholeness while we forgive their false projections. No greater adventure exists than courageous camaraderie with outcasts daring this interbeing! All conflict thus transforms undemocratic uneven ground perpetuating suffering into embrace vast enough for diverse realities held tenderly beyond surface threats they pose to identity. Such wholehearted communication magnetizes miraculous manifestation!

Thus concludes our exploration of conscious communication tools and techniques for enriching relationships at home, work and community contexts through mindful emotional wisdom, non-violent speech, addressing conflicts compassionately and the sacred power of vulnerable witnessing for healing and inspiration.

Chapter 10: Multidimensional Healing – Harmonizing Our Subtle Bodies

———

"Your subtle energy body stores the blueprint of your life purpose. When it's flooded with light, you feel inspired, confident and guided. When it's congested and low on energy, you lack clarity and doubt yourself." – Denise Linn

"Doctor, please help! Something is seriously wrong. I keep getting splitting migraines, chronic fatigue and burning nerves throughout my arms for months now... but countless tests show everything fine!" I pleaded tearfully at my wit's end as the medical expert stared baffled too at the inconclusive heap of blood reports and scans.

Sensing unseen root causes at play beyond detecting capabilities of modern hospitals, my grandmother intuitively took me to an indigenous shaman living remotely deep within an Amazon rainforest sanctuary. His wise crinkled eyes gazing intensely during sacred plant ceremonies saw what CT scans couldn't – my energetic field filled with torn holes leaking vitality... possibly from traumatic past life or ancestral imprints haunting cells unresolved needing psychic nourishment and cosmic surgery beyond vitamins! I still remember sighing huge relief after soul retrievals filling those gaps followed by nurturing my aura daily henceforth noticing radical resilience...

This pivotal realization that our beings are far more fascinating than biology alone reveals opened doorways for aligning natural wellbeing when isolated chemical quick fixes or fear-based surgeries limitedly treating disease symptoms but not holistic causes perpetuate exhaustion fighting universal flows. Let's explore our multidimensional anatomy and subtle healing arts that awaken extraordinary potentials!

10.1 Our Interconnected Energy Systems

Through the mystical lens, our fundamental life force stems from an intelligent awareness field – the unbounded eternal Consciousness animating existence itself. Mainstream science also confirms how invisible energy dynamics like gravity, electromagnetism and subtle quantum interconnectivities shape realities more fundamentally than dense physical matter.

Similarly, observing nature and our bodies under contemplative microscopes unveils the sublime contextual ocean in which tangible forms appear temporarily as fluid waves. Growth unfolds at more subtle planes first before consolidating physically. Like ice transforming to water then vaporized invisible mist before skies, consciousness utilises vehicles of perception interfacing formlessness to form for enrichment incarnating across kingdoms meaningfully.

Let's map key mystical energy structures developing our earthly sojourns and tools aligning their symbiotic synergy for wellbeing:

1. Physical Body: Our miraculous biological vessel composed of dense matter for anchoring spirit into diversity experience honoring sacred planet and collective healing. Mastering balance across vehicle parts unlocks optimal functioning for soul lessons chosen.

1. Pranic Body + Chakras: The vital life force network of 72,000 energy channels or nadis that distribute breath, anchor consciousness into body tissues, maintain cellular cohesion and immunity. Major hub centers are spinning bioenergetics chakra vortices aligning vertical energies flow between heaven and earth optimally like flesh lotuses blossoming consciousness through matter.

1. Mental Body: Our individualized field of thoughts, belief paradigms and reasoning – lens analyzing, recording and strategizing based on inputs, aspirations plus interpretations filtered through cultural worldviews and past life imprints. WIT educating emotional wisdom nurtures intuition guiding beyond inherited conditioning alone for expanded futures.

1. Astral Body: The subtle space where feelings, dream states and non physical connections operate like telepathy or mystical visions. Remembering techniques facilitate traversing these soulful domains more consciously conveying teachings to waking self instead of dismissing this nocturnal classroom.

1. Causal Body: Houses key blueprint codes of higher destiny and soul memory until each being awakens unfolding divine gifts through lifetime practice. Challenging conditions orchestrate to catalyze latent virtues. Once earth planes mastery integrates lessons fully, we transcend mortal coils unless volunteering again as awakened guides.

1. The 3 Granthi: Sanskrit for psychic knots that limit most human minds identifying rigidly with individual body rather than unity consciousness. Unwinding granthi through breath work and meditation gradually opens aware identity with cosmic Self beyond little me. We glimpse our eternal existence within infinite spirit understands death as shifting states.

THUS WE RECOGNIZE MULTIDIMENSIONAL presence ever evolving through vast interdependence, only notionally separated. Discovering keys harmonizing vehicles frees huge creative forces for flourishing and service!

10.2 Understanding the Chakra System

Chakras manifest where swirling channels of pranic currents cross forming concentrated energy hubs associated with endocrine glands, nervous plexus and organs clusters around a matching element controlling bodily and consciousness functions when balanced. Let's clarify the 7 main wheels:

1st Root Chakra – Located at base of spine governing sense of groundedness, survival priorities, elimination. Element earth.

2nd Sacral Chakra – Lower abdomen. Sensuality, intimacy, fluidity, creativity, reproduction. Element water.

3rd Solar Plexus- Stomach area. Willpower, self worth, humor, frontal authority. Element fire.

4th Heart Chakra – Chest region. Compassion. Unconditional unity experience. Circulates spiritual and human love. Element air.

5th Throat Chakra – Neck. Self expression, communication discernment, truth resonance.

6th Third Eye – Middle forehead. Intuition from beyond 5 senses data. Telepathic knowing and inner vision. Pineal gland site.

7th Crown Chakra – Top of head. Consciousness expansion into formless infinite freedom. Divine union.

Through practices balancing centers holistically e.g grounding with Kapalbhati cleansing stagnation across channels until prana flows smoothly elevating soul through purified nadis into crown bliss belying all worldly ambitions by self sufficient inner richness, we unlock incredible gifts like healing abilities, clairvoyance, unconditional love and fearless peace sourced from sacred innermost core instead of external conditions.

Chakra Medicine Menu For Alignment:

1) Embodied Movement – Tailor fitness from dense hopping to loose ecstatic dance for sending earthly to ethereal

2) Creative Arts – Sound, mudra, painting attuning vibrational fields

3) Crystals Grids – Mineralogy amplifying specific electromagnetic frequencies

4) Essential Oils – Botanical helpers balancing left/right reptilian brain

5) Sacred Geometry – mandala paintings reflecting innermost patterns

6) Light Language – Tonal lexicon beyond encoded cultural meaning

Thus we consciously transform bioelectricity for nourishing nervous system health, tranquility, effervescent inspiration and harmonious co-creation by respecting body's Brilliant vehicle!

10.3 Crystalline Consciousness

Human design reflecting natural glimmering gemstones and sequoia symmetry implies cosmic origins in celestial stardust. Our molecules mirror crystalline sacred geometry. Silica rich bones, collagen fibers,

DNA double helixes and cholesterol cellular gates demonstrate highly conductive capacities transmuting frequencies as kundalini flowering metamorphs life force currents amplified by geomancy.

Anthropologist suggest lemurian and atlantean ancestry where ethereally enhanced races coexisting as earth keepers. Traditions like Vastu Shastra explain building homes and temples aligning with planetary grid auspiciously elevated lifestyles beyond 3D confines by dimensional tunings with Pyramids os specific mineralogy embedding caches across continents as communication portals.

Modern crystal healing reviving ancient remembering focused not on physical properties but subtle energy consciousness programming quartz and gradients. Shamans mention each containing device spirits guardian consciousness willing embodiment allies cleansing toxic residue or restructuring light grids.

Wearing crystals intentionally programs high vibe transmission assimilating stellar wisdom. Building geodesic homes from quartz transfers consciousness into enlightened civilizations like Atlantis. Silicon saturation explains Indigenous downloading plant medicines, animal languages and ancestral future memories as crystalline blueprint reboots. We inhabit resonating monuments lifting generations through conscious stones!

10.4 Traversing the Planes

Beyond tangible realms perceived by limited senses, mystics across traditions traverse multi layered dimensions witnessing firsthand the infinitely creative way Source expresses conceiving unlimited diversity transcending mundane existence!

Through practices stabilizing subtle awareness like meditation, vision quests, past life regressions and psychotropic substances expanding perceptual bandwidth normally constrained biologically for survival optimization, seers penetrate veils filtering consciousness capacities to reveal profoundly varied planes inhabited by guides, ancestors, array of non human entities in radically enhanced states compared with our narrow slumber.

They furnish experiential legitimacy to wisdom traditions already mapping territories beyond Earth promising deathless soul continuity however temporarily forgetting when reincarnating until each soul thoroughly integrates lessons through matrix immersion uplifting collective vibration enough for graduation.

Planes clairvoyants commonly encounter include:

1) Physical forms perceptible to 5 senses familiar

2) Emotion plane feeling subtle sensations

3) Lower astral with ghosts traversing between births

4) Causal storing soul blueprints + past life memory

5) Buddhic realm permeated by unconditional unity

6) Nirvanic planes dissolving separate self entirely !

Through courageously navigating once considered supernatural dimensions beyond polarized categorization into normal or paranormal, pioneering mystics expand rigid flatland notions of personhood into multidimensional embodiment across interconnected planes compassionately respecting our simultaneous citizenship amid formless infinity forever playing besides temporal mortality.

10.5 Integrative Healing Modalities

Once recognizing body as brilliant bioelectric sensors manifesting universal flow dynamics impacting wellbeing, empowering practices consciously direct subtle energies for preventive and restorative care.

Let us honor cultural wisdom keepers who maintain holistic faculties beyond isolating disease pathology independent from natural context or root metaphysical causes. Integrating synergistic healing arts elevates practitioners and patients beyond roles into empowered embodied sovereigns reclaiming authority of radiant beings masterfully conducting inner ecosystem in harmony with Earth rhythms.

Regulation not domination allows cleaned vessels receive divine back into sacred embodiment on Earth. Gratitude for vehicle transporting precious soul current further ignites latent supernormal talents. Healing happens!

Beneficial modalities include:

Reiki- Channeling ki universal essence as intelligent�addressing energetic and emotional blocks holistically

Acupuncture/Marma- Correcting blocked meridians and vital nadis through strategic needles therapy

Naturopathy – Organic whole plant supplements in align with biorhythms

Osteopathy – Addressing structural manipulations easing trapped trauma and chronic tension

Ayurveda / Siddha – Customizing lifestyle and botanical alliesto balance metabolic mind body types

Shamanism – Retrieving fragmented soul aspects and releasing entity attachments

Psychedelics – Kernel doses unlocking trauma repression and stagnation for neural flexibility

Chapter 11: Understanding Life's Sacred Meaning and Raising Spirituality

"There are only two ways to live your life. One is as though nothing is a miracle. The other is as though everything is a miracle." – Albert Einstein

I jolted awake at 3am drenched in angst-ridden sweat after another apocalyptic climate nightmare helplessly witnessing beloved forests burning as friendships deteriorated clashes over contrasting worldviews. Staggeringdc despairingly towards the bathroom contemplating how destructively humanity poisons perfectly balanced ecosystems spawning more social disconnection, I paused gaping awe at the sheer iridescent beauty of a simple spider glimmering near the mirror under moonlight like a celestial guardian angel beckoning silent cosmic reassurance...

In that ordinary yet miraculous moment beyond usual perceptions, something deep reminded hidden order weaves chaos into rebirths opportunity. I understood life's suffering – my conflicting roles juggling spiritual creativity against capitalist demands – as essential ingredients for awakening into empowered vision sourcing harmony instead of fatalism.

Suddenly sacred meaning glimmered subtly everywhere awaiting discovered mystery! From intricate fractal snowflakes to the perplexing phenomenon of infinity signs manifesting synchronistic ally through reflections in puddles, tea leaves and window condensation each morning I now noticed winking design intelligence thrumming creation's multidimensional tapestry no more accidental than clockwork...

This chapter summarizes why we incarnate in biological bodies, clarifies cultural conditioning clouding natural clarity and suggests impactful techniques maturing limited consciousness into awakened wonder again fully aligned with spiritual truth sourcing existence itself!

11.1 Life's Deeper Purpose: Soul Evolution

Mainstream notions portray us as randomly evolved primate gene pools awaking one day on average universe floating amidst empty cosmological vastness awaiting reaction with no definitive meaning...

But across history and cultures, our wisest philosophers, shamans and saints illuminate profound teleological purpose permeating existence itself as Brahman dreaming into form. Reality unfolds like spectacular play tapping latent potential for new heights of imagination and ecstatic love as consciousness adventures through the cosmos experiencing itself.

We incarnate as fractals of eternal Awareness into delicately biodesigned mortal vessels allowing soul maturation through learning cycles not possible remaining eternally merged with Divine Light as mere passive homogenous droplets.

Catalyzed by desire for novel participation, Source plunges as individuated rays into matrices of limitation strengthened and polished gradually by experiential friction until reflecting completely purified back to unbounded wholeness – Buddha nature ready for blissful re-absorption having enjoyed bewildering display of relativity and unity expressing through multitude diverse ephemeral forms questing their way back home through inner-directed flowering.

Through incarnation, consciousness embeds wisdom deeply felt into multiple being bodies to appreciate the great blessing of existence again never taken for granted unconsciously.

Our highest purpose thus lies realizing nonduality beneath illusion of separation until compassion overflows serving family, species and planet wholeheartedly.

11.2 Waking Up From Cultural Conditioning and Matrix Manipulation

However clearer existence's goal focused on conscious evolution through loving co-creation and synergetic harmony mimicking nature's fractal patterns itself, few stray outside rigid tribal mental paradigms imprinted since birth by families, education systems and authoritarian structures unconsciously perpetuating cycles of fear-run greed, scarcity and competition sabotaging our cooperative flowering seeded naturally.

Cultural trance perpetuates through...

1. Valuing Comparison & Conformity

We get habituated judging daily successes narrowly based on materialistic ownership, beauty and status signifiers appreciated by equally conditioned peers rather than soul mentorship nurturing strengths boiled uniquely when young steam gets forced into collective molds undermining authentic becoming.

1. Worshipping Authority

Questioning parents, elderly, scriptures and governments feels flippant though many regulations standardizing "proper living" violate ecological sensitivity, human rights and heart truths that accumulated oppression births movements upholding justice despite steep persecution initially.

1. Prioritizing Profits Over Ethics

Capitalism's competitive corner-cutting business approaches demand focusing corporate efficiency maximizing financial gains by hidden socioenvironmental externalizing cost until crisis corrects but operational models could uplift humanity's cooperative genius sourcing sustainability.

We uncritically adopt narrow worldviews seeking safety within regimental walls but blossom from releasing minds beyond manipulation by mastering awareness.

11.3 Steps to Increase Spiritual Consciousness

"It is no measure of health to be well adjusted to a profoundly sick society." ~ Jiddu Krishnamurti

We clear conditioned delusion (Maya) by...

1. Examining Implicit Biases

Ingrained tendency automatically favoring certain groups while reacting fearfully towards different "others" perpetuates perceived separation threatening wholeness. Notice prejudice by compassionately questioning reactive impressions repeated exposure unravels.

1. Allowing Diverse Experience

Beyond familiar zones and friend demographics, stretch comfort bubbles respectfully befriending cultural opposites appreciating exotic wisdom traditions, alternate healing systems and unfamiliar communities. Bridge understanding through courageous vulnerability.

1. Balancing Opinions with Facts

Differentiate subjective viewpoints, projections and theories from empirical evidence analysis when assessing validity of beliefs before internalizing or spreading information online. Verify supporting data and contextual nuance reducing exaggeration.

1. Fact-Checking Reliable Sources

Responsibly trace independent multimedia press, scholarly reference and historical documentation conveying balanced multiperspective debate on issues instead of opinionated infotainment, celebrity analysis or sensational headlines propagating agendas through attention hijacking without grounded substance.

1. Embracing Subjectivity While Seeking Objectivity

Recognize no ultimate monopoly on truth exists beyond situational relativity across constantly evolving unpredictable contexts. But through reconciling information gathered from discrete explorative questioning, factual reliability and intuitive coherence indicators, we sustainably approximate collective decision making productivity guided by gnosis insight.

11.4 Remembering Our Divine Blueprint

While mastering precious human birth through mindfulness sharpening witness clarity here and now absolutely establishes priority improving relationships and service legacy immediate generations, recalling origin soul memories from past incarnations or galactic consciousness channeled through psychic mediums explains foundational forces propelling incarnations now for profound healing giving context to conditions.

Many hypnotically regress subjects report selecting struggle themes for destruction/ reconstruction breaking karmic cycles like...

1) Healer lifetimes to balance violence inflicted as warring knight upon innocents

2) Creative work redeeming suppression by religious torture silencing feminine divinity expressions as witch

3) Leadership correcting the abusive authoritarian misuse of power from opposing side of marginalization

4) Athletic instead of academic accelerating strengths dismissed by intellectual family

5) Nature conservation healing pillaging of resources for industrial greed

We orient meaning and heal trauma by understanding specific scenarios orchestrate redemption awakening latent virtues. Core soul blueprint anchors purpose!

11.5 Allowing Our Unique Spirit to Guide Life

"Let yourself be silently drawn by the stronger pull of what you really love." ~ Rumi

Once analyzing beliefs and childhood imprinting limiting behaviors perpetuating collective dysfunction melts by fiery blossoming of presence beyond seeking external conformity/VALIDATION as peaceful seed untouched by swirling storming surrounding, we effortlessly emit soul frequencies through natural resonance in harmony attracting tribe sharing truth values beyond surface persona.

Gradually we decode matrix illusions as cooperative playground for creative exploration like musical improvisation dreaming reality into dynamic form by courageously wielding focused imagination, unapologetic vision seeded by great spirit.

No longer hostage to other's projections but radically responsible self-parent inner innocent vulnerability, we lead by humble example not authoritarian demands. Lotus gently breaks surface then vibrantly blooms in own time by inward authority not outward chaos.

At ease with not-yet-knowing possibilities mysteriously become unquestionably obvious next steps guided from within as destiny. We finally fertilize soul gifts long abandoned for routine security that expression was luxury not priority postponed perpetually for retirement freedom that never came.

The ordinary becomes sacred as life opens Invitation sending secret scented clues guiding purpose. Natural inheritance Stirs destiny!

We shine blessings by simply being amazing beings incarnate travelling together, reminding in darkest coldest seasons, eternal spring patiently glows within reaching for sunlight.

Chapter 12: Integrating Our Sacred Awakening – Roadmap for Conscious Living and Remembering Our True Essence

"When you recover who you are, you recover your destiny." – T.D. Jakes

As we near the closing of this transformative journey unveiling the mystical truth at the heart of existence behind external chaos and cultural facades, you might feel both disoriented and dynamized by parallel revelations patiently waiting behind veils...

Like any rebirth, a period of integration helps anchor expansion into practical wisdom for application in relationships, work-life flow and community cooperation seeding systemic flowering. Let us review key lessons for embodying higher truth as teachers might summarize intensive classroom learnings before sending eager students out into the world for impactful contribution!

The 4 Cornerstones of Conscious Living

1. Committing to Self-Discovery

Staying curious about inner worlds beyond conditioning stories opens us to receive deeper soul insights guiding aligned action intuitively through synchronistic support.

1. Mastering Mindfulness

Beyond fleeting mystical glimpses, a dedicated practice of witnessing focus grounds unshakable presence to ride changing phenomena without attachment. Equanimity flourishes meeting all emotions and situations with compassion.

1. Living Aligned Purpose

Clarifying core inspirations and innate talents allows passionate path to flow through us abundantly uplifting lives far beyond surface identities by unleashing creative potential.

1. Seed Conscious Community

Cross-pollinate understanding beyond silos and demographics that limit diversity wisdom. Practice unconditional listening without bias, have courage to address shadow projections sabotaging unity and lead collaborative actions seeded for 7 generations.

Remembering Our True Essence

"You are not a drop in the ocean. You are the entire ocean in a drop." ~ Rumi

Strip away peripheral layers of stepping stone roles – child, lover, professional or ageing body – witness absolute essence existing at core ever untouched by transient costumes or conditions...

Our blissful true nature is unbounded Buddha or Christ consciousness – awakened constant awareness containing the cosmos, freely shapeshifting across myriad multidimensional experiences as all beings throughout creation like glimmering diamond facets...Concealing and revealing the Great Mystery through myriad ego lenses till fascination culminates finally into unified abiding nondual recognition when prodigal sons/daughters accomplish full redemption arc after countless trials and errors to interview perspective holding all stories simultaneously with empathy not judgement.

This culminating mystical revelation sets initiates truly free into eternal divine play without clinging attachment! Gravity no longer compels identity into rigid roles, we float unrestricted through myriad experiential possibilities interacting across planes endlessly surprising ourselves as efficiently as Infinite Beingness delights creating, preserving and dissolving existence!

When ripe fruits unclench fists desperately clutching fleeting phenomena for security, we organically surrender mortal ghosts to cross triumphantly into omnipresent implicate order where unlimited synchronicity and cosmic support manifests anew in each moment to nourish destiny beyond wildest dreams!

No separate self remains to claim awakening, only infinite delight dancing, creating, forgiving and forgetting perpetually through ever changing forms from stillness into dynamism without exhausting eternally blissful transcendental source which we all already inhabit.

The only controller of cosmic game disappears last!

Thus concludes our adventurous exploration into embodying awakened consciousness fully within myriad realms spanning relative to absolute truth!

THE END